Barney Frank and the Law of Unintended Consequences

Barney Frank and the Law of Unintended Consequences

◆

How the Frank Amendment Helped Terrorists get Legal Visas

Chuck Morse

iUniverse, Inc.
New York Lincoln Shanghai

Barney Frank and the Law of Unintended Consequences
How the Frank Amendment Helped Terrorists get Legal Visas

Copyright © 2005 by Charles A. Morse

iUniverse books may be ordered through booksellers or by contacting:

iUniverse
2021 Pine Lake Road, Suite 100
Lincoln, NE 68512
www.iuniverse.com
1-800-Authors (1-800-288-4677)

ISBN-13: 978-0-595-35948-6 (pbk)
ISBN-13: 978-0-595-80401-6 (ebk)
ISBN-10: 0-595-35948-5 (pbk)
ISBN-10: 0-595-80401-2 (ebk)

Printed in the United States of America

This book is dedicated to the memory of the victims of the 9/11 terrorists.

Contents

Aiding and Abetting

When turned into actions, well-intentioned ideas often have unintended consequences. This book is primarily about an ill-conceived idea that became a federal law, which contributed to the deaths of 3,000 people on September 11, 2001. The consequences of the 1990 amendment to the Immigration and Nationality Act (1.), whose chief sponsor was Massachusetts Congressman Barney Frank, emerged 11 years later when radical Islamic terrorists, having legally obtained visas to enter this country as a result of that law, hijacked four passenger planes and turned them into missiles. The terrorists used those planes filled with commuters to blow up the Twin Towers in Manhattan and a part of the Pentagon.

When a bad idea becomes the law of the land the consequences are often borne by an entire nation and can have a profound effect on the course of history. Barney Frank sponsored the immigration legislation known as the Frank amendment because he actually believed that the American government ought to be legally prevented from denying visas to foreigners who espouse unpopular political or philosophical views or who are affiliated with unpopular causes. He believed that the FBI and CIA should be prevented from sharing information about aspects of the background of visa applicants. (2.) He was motivated by the dubious conviction that a federal law was necessary to protect foreigners applying for visas from the possibility of discrimination.

The issue of discrimination should be viewed as irrelevant to questions regarding the issuance of visas to foreigners. Constitutional protections, the Civil Rights Act and other civil rights legislation apply to American citizens not foreigners seeking visas. The Constitution protects rights such as free speech and other civil rights in America. There is no such thing as a civil right for an individual from a foreign country to visit the United States or to visit any sovereign state. The Frank amendment furthered a trend toward applying domestic civil rights codes to visa applicants, which severely compromised national security.

1

Frank also sponsored an amendment, which called for the setting up of a Board of Visa Appeals within the State Department. (3.) State Department officials predicted at the time that the appeals process would make it more difficult for officials stationed in American embassies in foreign capitals to deny visas. Trained officials would no longer be able to deny visas based solely upon their own professional judgment.

The cumbersome roadblock made it more likely that an embassy official, much like the post Frank amendment INS official, would over time prefer avoiding the hassle and the possible risk to reputation involved in denying a visa without compelling evidence. Two examples of the consequences of this law was the ease in which two of the 9/11 hijackers, Marwan al-Shehi and Hani Hanjour, received their visas at the American Embassy in the United Arab Emirates. Frank's concern that an embassy official might discriminate against a foreign visa applicant resulted in the wrongful admission of hardened criminals.

The Frank amendment is the centerpiece of no less than thirteen amendments to the Immigration and Nationality Act sponsored by Frank between 1981 and 2001. (4.) The central legacy of his involvement in immigration matters over two decades in Congress is the presence of disciplined and well-organized networks of terrorist sleeper cells and support groups that have become embedded in America. Besides causing death and destruction, the presence of the terrorists has altered our way of life. We must now cope with the necessary restrictions on the ease with which we travel. We must now live with heightened terrorist alerts and a fear of large gatherings. We've had to accept laws that restrict certain liberties that were previously taken for granted. Our government must now deal with a crisis that was largely created by the inept meddling of Barney Frank in immigration policy.

Frank's testimony at a hearing of the House Select Committee on Homeland Security on August 17, 2004 sheds some light on the mindset behind the chief sponsor of the Frank amendment. The subject discussed at that hearing was "toward a paradigm for homeland security information sharing." In his testimony to the committee, Frank expressed concern over FBI agents investigating the possibility that terrorists might strike the Democratic or Republican National Conventions held that summer in Boston and Manhattan. There was a heightened concern around those enormous gatherings and the government had a solid reason to suspect that they could be targeted for terrorism. FBI agents were interviewing people as to whether they had witnessed any suspicious goings on in the vicinity of the national conventions. Frank rhetorically asked whether the FBI was "that deep in extra agents that they've got people with nothing else to do for the summer."

In his testimony, Frank revealed that his motivation for sponsoring the Frank amendment and the other immigration amendments was based on a false premise when he made reference to federal guidelines that "took account to the reality that suspicion of 'terrorism,' like suspicion of 'subversion,' could lead to making individuals targets for investigation more because of their beliefs than because of their acts….I'm wondering if you think…Frank dramatically stated…have we gotten that out of our system? Is it coming back?"

The reference to "suspicion of subversion" and to something that we should have worked "out of our system" was a clear reference to the Congressional investigations of the 1940's and 1950's that dealt with the question of Soviet influence in the United States. Those investigations, generally referred to as the McCarthy era hearings, had absolutely nothing whatsoever to do with Frank's visa legislation, which was crafted decades later. Comparing the two is like comparing apples and oranges.

Those investigations looked into whether American citizens, particularly those who were government employees in sensitive positions, were actively lending support to the government of Josef Stalin at the expense of the United States. While I would argue that those investigations were warranted, as history has borne out, nevertheless serious mistakes were made in terms of falsely accusing innocent American citizens who held leftist views of aiding a foreign enemy. There are many examples of civil liberties having been impinged upon during that period and I don't believe anyone would want to see a return to that type of government excess. The Frank amendment, however, is extraordinary government excess, one that has caused irreparable harm and human suffering far exceeding the unfortunate over-reactions of the McCarthy era.

The controversy surrounding the McCarthy era hearings was that they impinged on the rights of American citizens not foreigners applying for visas or visiting this country on a visa. Most Americans back then opposed granting visas to foreign Communists and that included luminaries such as Senators John F. Kennedy, Hubert H. Humphrey, and Lyndon B. Johnson. The government understood as a routine matter that entry would be denied to known or suspected enemies.

It should be noted that the Congressional committee in question, the House Committee on un-American Activities, was established in the late 1930's at the request of President Franklin D. Roosevelt for the purpose of investigating the possibility that Nazi agents and sympathizers were engaging in subversive activities. It was only toward the end of World War II, with the impending defeat of the Nazi regime, that the House Committee turned its attention to Communism.

This was during the post World War II period, a time when Soviet Communism posed as a substantial threat to this country and to world peace. The Soviet Union had consolidated an iron grip over Eastern Europe in the late 1940's, China had fallen to the Communists in 1949, South Korea was invaded in 1950, and the Soviet Union had detonated a nuclear bomb in the early 1950's.

On March 5, 1946, Winston Churchill made note of these developments in a speech he delivered at Westminster College in Fulton, Missouri when he spoke of an "Iron Curtain" descending across the heart of Europe. It has now been acknowledged by responsible people that Communism was responsible for the murders of tens of millions of people and for starving and oppressing hundreds of millions worldwide as it occupied more than half of the surface of the globe.

None of these developments should be viewed as an excuse for an American government to falsely question the loyalty of a single American citizen or to hold an American citizen up for ridicule for expressing a political point of view. The United States did not sacrifice the lives of tens of thousands of heroic men in uniform who valiantly fought wars against Nazism and Communism so that our government could proceed to assume some of the trappings of those defeated authoritarian systems.

When he crafted his legislation, Frank thought he was helping left-wing applicants enter the country but instead, because of the heavy-handed nature of the legislation he crafted, which forbids exclusion based on opinion or political affiliations, he swung the door open to anti-American radical Islamic Jihadists. While railing against those who express concern over "subversion," Frank made it possible for foreign subversives, members of groups such as Hamas and Hizbollah, to come here to raise funds for "charities," foment violence, recruit new members, and eventually blow up the economic icon of America, The World Trade Center.

Except in the imagination of Barney Frank, none of the history of those Congressional investigations has anything to do with forcing the government by law to grant visas to potential foreign enemies. I reiterate, the responsibility of the House Committee on un-American Activities was to primarily investigate the activities of American citizens, not foreign applicants for visas, and in doing so they went overboard. The government had the right to fully investigate foreign visa applicants, and to consider their ideology in that investigation, before the Frank amendment. The Frank amendment and accompanying legislation granted rights to foreigners who sought entry, rights that had never existed before and that were manufactured out of whole cloth, and by implication, those foreigners were able to exercise those rights once they ensconced themselves inside the United States. This had never been done before up until that point and for good reason.

Frank's warped concern over immigration matters began 24 years ago in 1981, his first term in Congress, when he sponsored H.R. 5287, an amendment to greatly expand the teacher and student visa program. (5.) He did this using the argument that increased numbers of foreign College students would contribute greatly to the American economy and society and, in many cases, the foreign students would settle here and enrich us with their professional skills. The benefit of foreign students attending American institutions of learning is, of course, undeniable and not disputed.

The problem with the sweeping student visa legislation sponsored by Frank, and passed into law years later in another guise, was that it loosened restrictions and the ability to monitor foreign college "students" such as Mohammed Atta, the reputed ringleader of the 9/11 terrorists, who easily obtained a student visa. The new student visa program would make it easier for, as theoretical examples, a North Korean "student" to attend an American university in order to study nuclear physics or a Palestinian "student" attending an institution of higher learning in order to study explosives.

Student visa requirements became so lax that by the late 1990's Mohammed Atta and several other 9/11 terrorists actually had their visas changed from visitor status to that of student under the assumption that it was less likely authorities would be inclined to check up on a "student." Hani Hanjour, one of the terrorist pilots on 9/11, obtained his student visa while not even bothering to enroll in a College.

In 1995, after American Brandeis student Alisa Flatow was murdered by the Islamic Jihad in the Gaza Strip, it was revealed that Sami al-Arian, the alleged ringleader of Islamic Jihad, had easily obtained a teaching visa to the University of Florida. Congressman Frank's original bill, H.R. Amendment 5287, had started the ball rolling toward the weakening of the process of monitoring foreign students. Reportedly marbled within the vast majority of legitimate foreign teachers and students studying in this country were supporters of terrorist groups and operatives from rogue nations.

Other amendments to the Immigration and Nationality act sponsored by Frank include a bill that made it possible for an already deported foreign convict to come back into this country to appeal a deportation, a law that is known as the Family Reunification Act. (6.) The intent of this law was to help a resident alien who ran afoul of the law decades ago but who had since paid his debt to society and had become an honest citizen, who was being threatened with deportation many years later for the old crime. There is no controversy surrounding the assertion that a person in this circumstance should not be deported. The problem again arises over the sweeping nature of legislation that unintentionally swung the door open to a broad range of foreign criminals who had previously been convicted and deported for recent crimes and who would be able to apply for re-entry.

Congressman Frank pushed for a law that would grant temporary visas to foreigners with AIDS. Such a law would perhaps constitute the first time in recorded history in which a nation would be required to grant visas to individuals with a dangerous and contagious disease. The effect of such a reckless law would be to place gay American men, already burdened with the AIDS health crisis, at a greater risk of contracting this dread disease. Again, exceptions could have been made in specific cases for specific applicants rather than the crafting of sweeping legislation which would effectively hold the nation's door open to anyone with AIDS.

While gutting centuries old immigration laws, which provided security from foreign terrorists, Frank at the same time sponsored a bill that substantially cut

CIA funding during the Clinton administration. This resulted in severe CIA budget cuts in 1997. The cuts went forward despite dire warnings from Clinton's CIA director, George Tenet, of an ominous terrorist threat. The sponsoring of a series of laws that hamstrung the government's ability to deny visas to potential terrorists while at the same time the sponsorship of a law that cut funding for the agency in charge of investigating the terrorist threat was, to use a British understatement, unwise.

Justice must be brought to bear on behalf of the 3,000 people who were mercilessly killed at the hands of the terrorists on 9/11. Understanding the circumstances that contributed to that day, and what actually went wrong, is the only means of finding a long-term remedy to an American immigration system that is out of control.

The Frank amendment and the other immigration amendments sponsored by the Congressman and others involve a conscious and deliberate agenda, one that contradicts historical norms of international law and custom as well as basic common sense. This is not a story about negligence, carelessness, or stupidity. This is a story about the prolonged and concerted effort of a particular politician who is described by many liberals as one of the most intelligent members of Congress. Congressman Frank did not act alone. Other likeminded Congressmen, both Democrat and Republican, voted yes on his immigration legislation over the years and sponsored similar legislation. While Frank was the leading sponsor of this type of legislation, nevertheless there is plenty of blame to go around.

One of the cautionary lessons that ought to be derived from the wreckage of the Frank amendment and its accompanying laws is that the number one priority of this or of any responsible government ought to be the protection of the lives and property of its citizens from foreign intrigue and domestic threat. In order to wield any moral authority or to generate even a modicum of trust and respect from the citizenry, governments must assume responsibility for safeguarding the most basic and most fundamental function of national sovereignty, which is the protection of the citizenry.

This basic principle is the natural right and moral responsibility of all nations and the cornerstone of freedom and individual rights. Laws that contradict this most basic notion contradict the principle of the rule of law. Political philosopher

George Santayana said it best, "Those who cannot remember the past are condemned to repeat it."

The devastatingly misguided policies created by the Frank amendment, and the philosophy that rationalizes them has wrought terrible consequences on the lives of individuals and on the nation as a whole. In this Congressional session, the nation must undo the damage of the past three decades and quit unwittingly aiding and abetting the sworn enemies of America.

Opening the Floodgates

I was first made aware of Massachusetts Congressman Barney Frank's long and persistent record of meddling into immigration matters in 2004, during my own campaign against him for Congress in the 4th congressional district of Massachusetts. In the course of the campaign, a supporter emailed me excerpts from the just released New York Times bestseller "Why America Slept—The Failure to Prevent 9/11" by former Wall Street lawyer, self described liberal investigative journalist and author Gerald Posner.

Gerald Posner is an award-winning author of eight books, a frequent guest commentator on TV, and a writer for the New York Times, The New Yorker, Newsweek, the Wall Street Journal and U.S.News and World Report. Posner wrote this expose to expound on events that led up to the terrorist attack on the World Trade Center and the Pentagon. This was not some right-wing book, but rather a New York Times bestseller soon to be made into a Showtime miniseries, published by Ballantine Books, a subsidiary of Simon and Schuster.

Congressman Frank is specifically mentioned in this book, now available in a paperback edition, in the following excerpt (page 17-18): (1.)

"Ronald Reagan might have named the Soviet Union as his primary foreign policy nemesis, but Islamic extremists were getting his attention and increasingly making the United States look vulnerable and weak. From the 1983 bombing of the marine barracks in Lebanon that killed 241 soldiers to the 1985 hijackings of TWA flight 847 and the cruise liner Achille Lauro, Middle Eastern terror was now on the White House's priority agenda.

"Senior CIA officers complained to the president's national security team about their frustration with the FBI and warned that America was vulnerable to Islamic terrorists entering on legal visas and setting up sleeper cells.

"Reagan responded in September 1986 by forming an interagency task force, the Alien Border Control Committee (ABCC), whose purpose was to block entry of suspected terrorists and to deport militants who either had come into the country illegally or had overstayed their visas. The CIA and FBI joined the ABCC effort.

"Six months after its formation, the ABCC had its first notable success. The CIA tipped off the FBI to a group of suspected Palestinian terrorists in Los Angeles. The Bureau arrested eight men. But instead of being lauded, the Bureau and the Agency came under harsh attack from civil liberties groups who argued that the ABCC should be banned from using any information the CIA gained from the government's routine processing of visa requests.

"Congressman Barney Frank, the Massachusetts Democrat who was a strong advocate of protecting civil liberties, led a successful effort to amend the Immigration and Nationality Act so that membership in a terrorist group was no longer sufficient to deny a visa.

"Under Frank's amendment, which seems unthinkable post 9/11, a visa could only be denied if the government could prove that the applicant had committed an act of terrorism. Rendered toothless by the Frank amendment, the Reagan Administration had virtually no way to block entry visas even when there was information linking the individuals to terrorist groups."

Mark Riebling, the editorial director of the Manhattan Institute for Policy Research is the author of "*Wedge: From Pearl Harbor to 9/11—How the secret war between the FBI and CIA has endangered National Security.*" Riebling also made reference in his book to the Frank amendment claiming that the Congressman had prevented the Alien Border Control Committee, what Riebling described as a "special FBI-CIA unit" from fulfilling its vital mission. Riebling wrote that because of the Frank amendment, the government "*could not deport known members of terrorist groups; the government had to show that an individual had actually committed a terrorist act*"(2.)

Craig McDonald, staff writer and now editor of the Columbus Ohio based community newspaper "ThisWeek" wrote the following about the Frank amendment in his review of Gerald Posner's book in an article entitled "Posner's Terrorism Study Engages, Enrages." (9/18/03) "*With that stroke of the pen, Frank essentially opened the floodgates to terrorists looking to operate, foment and fund-raise on U.S. soil.*"

R. James Woolsey, Director of the CIA during the Clinton Administration, reviewed Posner's book for the Wall Street Journal (10/21/03). He made reference to the Frank amendment without mentioning the Congressman by name. Woolsey wrote that Congress had made it *"illegal to deny visas to members of terrorist groups."* In the article, Woolsey described the Frank amendment as one of the underlying causes of 9/11. In his synopsis, the former CIA director made reference to the communication breakdown between the agencies when he wrote, *"The CIA and FBI fail to talk to one another; both fail to talk to the Immigration and Naturalization Service or the State Department."*

Paul Mulshine, columnist for the New Jersey paper "The Star Ledger," wrote about the Frank amendment in "Terrorist Backers In; Common Sense Out (9/14/04)." The Congressman was interviewed for the article and he had no problem acknowledging: *"I did sponsor legislation…that ended the practice of excluding people from our country because we disagree with their political views."* The Frank amendment would create a strange set of circumstances in which the government would be legally required to grant visas to foreign Nazi skinheads, or racist or anti-Semitic agitators, even though most of the citizenry would *"disagree with their political views."* In fact, after the Frank amendment became law, this is exactly what happened.

The Congressman, however, sought to exonerate himself in a letter to the editor of the Star Ledger, in response to an earlier column by Mulshine, in which made reference to the Frank amendment when he wrote *"Mulshine asks what I was thinking when I sponsored a bill that precluded immigration officials from refusing entry to foreigners with admitted terrorist connections. The answer is nothing since I never sponsored any such legislation."*

Terrorist connections are hard to prove very few applicants for visas would admit to such connections. The espousal of terrorist ideas would no longer be considered as a reason for denying a visa to a foreigner seeking to visit under the restrictions put forth by the Frank amendment. Proving terrorist connections requires hard work and coordination between agencies, which broke down after the Frank amendment stripped the ABCC of its ability to function. After the Frank amendment, government officials would no longer be able to exercise their judgment or depend upon their well-trained instincts. Judging a visa applicant based upon their stated views and opinions, regardless of how inflammatory, would now be viewed as prejudicial or politically incorrect.

For the column, Mulshine interviewed Jessica Vaughn from the Center for Immigration Studies who noted that American immigration officials are told that they can't even consider political opinions when issuing visas. *"You can never refuse somebody on those grounds,"* Vaughn told Mulshine. *"The person practically has to come in and say, 'Yeah, I was going to blow up whatever.' And that might not be enough if they didn't do it."*

The Alien Border Control Committee (ABCC) was created by the Reagan administration, at the behest of intelligence operatives, to help prevent suspected terrorists or terrorist supporters from entering the United States. Once here, if a resident alien became a suspect, the ABCC would have been in charge of helping security, intelligence, and law enforcement agencies coordinate a detention and deportation on the basis that the suspect had violated a technical immigration rule. The primary means of accomplishing this vital work was that the ABCC was supposed to serve as a communications conduit.

The law enforcement principle applied here was the same time-honored approach used by the FBI in the apprehension of alleged members of organized crime. It had been proven to be the case that the best and surest way of detaining an organized crime suspect was over a technical violation. Perhaps the most famous example of this approach involved legendary Chicago gangster Al Capone, who was implicated in large numbers of crimes including murder. He would eventually be arrested, convicted, and imprisoned on a minor tax evasion charge.

President Reagan issued National Security Decision Directive (NSDD) 207 on January 20, 1986 thus creating the ABCC in an attempt *"to coordinate the full weight of the government's…resources in a campaign against radical Islamic guerrillas and similar groups."* (3.) In particular, the ABCC directive called for the deportation of *"PLO activists who have violated their visa status…."* (4.) The Palestine Liberation Organization (PLO) was the terrorist precursor to Hamas, al Queda, and other groups, and was one of the most deadly international terrorist organizations of the mid 1980's.

The FBI had been gathering evidence at the time that indicated that the PLO was in the process of infiltrating the country and was ratcheting up its activities within the United States, particularly in the Los Angeles area. There was a considerable and well-founded fear within the intelligence community that the PLO was facilitating the creation of terror cells, raising funds for so-called "charities" operating overseas, propagandizing and recruiting locally, and harassing the Muslim American community.

Frank introduced his amendment in response to the arrest, coordinated by the ABCC, of eight Palestinian resident aliens in Los Angeles in 1986 who were suspected members of the Popular Front for the Liberation of Palestine (PFLP). The shadowy, ultra leftist, Syrian-based PFLP is an offshoot of the PLO. The PFLP had already been implicated in numerous assassinations and bombings and had spearheaded the infamous 1976 hijacking of Air France flight 139 from Athens in which 105 Jewish passengers were herded off a passenger jet at the Entebbe Airport in Uganda, at the behest of Ugandan Dictator Idi Amin.

Idi Amin's plan was to kill all the Jewish hostages. The non-Jewish hostages were released. Israeli commandos, headed by Yonatan Netanyahu, brother of future Israeli Prime Minister Binyamin Netanyahu, heroically rescued the hostages from the clutches of Amin and the leftist terrorists. Yonatan Netanyahu was killed in the spectacular rescue mission. The terrorists murdered Dora Bloch, an elderly Jewish woman who had a heart attack before the rescue mission and had to be left behind. Bloch was murdered in her hospital bed as an act of revenge.

The eight suspected members of the PFLP, all resident aliens, were arrested in Los Angeles as a result of the work of the ABCC. The men maintained that they were involved in raising money for "humanitarian" purposes (such as to support clinics and hospitals on the West Bank and Gaza), and were doing nothing more than holding educational "seminars" and distributing Palestinian magazines. One of the Palestinian men arrested, Khader Hamide, was on record as having spoken at a fundraiser in which he called for contributions *"for the combatants in Lebanon and on the West Bank. The revolution requires support."* (5.)

Congressman Frank filed the Frank amendment in reaction to those arrests (6.) and its passage stopped the work of the ABCC dead in its tracks just as the enterprise was getting off the ground. The result was a return by the FBI and CIA to the status quo ante, the same lack of coordination that had existed before the

ABCC was created. According to the 9/11 Commission Report issued in 2003, this communication breakdown was the primary cause of the unpreparedness on 9/11. The government was already aware of the problem of terrorist infiltration and the need to coordinate a response at least as far back as 1986, which was the reason why Reagan had tried to establish the ABCC.

After the Frank amendment had gutted the ABCC in the late 1980's, the terrorists began to systematically infiltrate America. Trends in the 1990's indicate that the terrorists got the message put forth by the Frank amendment loud and clear and that message was "come on in, the water's fine." The FBI and CIA went back to rivalry and infighting and INS officials became reluctant to judge an applicant based on ideology so as not to violate the new law.

Potential foreign terrorists and those who would support their activities would henceforth be able to gain easy entry into this country where they would proceed to operate with a relatively free hand under the protection of the law. This phenomenon accelerated after the Frank amendment went into effect and culminated on Tuesday, September 11, 2001. The effects of that catastrophe continue to reverberate today and the threat of terrorist activity remains ever present.

The equivalent of Reagan's ABCC would eventually be resurrected with the passage of the post 9/11 USA Patriot Act and the creation of the U.S. Department of Homeland Security. This would occur only after the devastation of 9/11 and over a decade after the ABCC was stymied by the Frank amendment. During those intervening years, untold numbers of terrorists were reportedly able to infiltrate into this country relatively undetected. Today, there is a very real threat that terrorist sleeper cells are amongst us and are quietly waiting for their marching orders. Since 9/11, the FBI has uncovered several of these terror cells.

Incredibly, Barney Frank, the chief sponsor of the law that had greatly contributed to the problem, became a member of the Congressional Committee on Homeland Security. He was subsequently removed from that committee a few weeks after the 2004 election. As his opponent for Congress in Massachusetts, I had called for his resignation from that committee during the campaign. I had made the Frank amendment an issue and had brought the issue up to several key members of Congress and their staffs. I had debated the issue with the Congressman during televised debates.

Congressman Frank, in response to my accusation said that his motive in sponsoring the Frank amendment was to remedy what he considered to be an inappropriate Cold War era law. The law in question, the 1950's era McCarran-Walter Act, was written with the intent of denying visas to foreigners with suspected connections to communist regimes. The law had recently been invoked to deny a visa to Columbian communist novelist Gabriel Garcia Marquez. Frank mentioned the case of the novelist, a close associate of Cuban communist dictator Fidel Castro, as an example of what he considered to be an injustice committed as a result of the McCarran-Walter act.

The American Communist "Peoples Daily World" had noted in an article written in the 1980's, during the debate over the Frank amendment that a *"bill by Rep. Barney Frank (D-Mass.), HR-1280, now before the House Judiciary Committee, would further reduce grounds for exclusion, eliminating, for example, the ban on representatives of "communist-dominated labor organizations"*(6.) The Daily World article complained that the AFL-CIO was opposed to Congressman Frank's inclusion of foreign communist labor organizers in his bill. It should be noted that by opposing the position taken by both the Communist Daily Worker and by Congressman Frank on this issue, the AFL-CIO was advocating in the best interests of both American labor and of the nation as a whole.

In an essay written and signed by Barney Frank, and posted on his official congressional website, October 10, 2001, four weeks after 9/11, entitled "Barney Frank's Views on the Terrorism Bill" (appendix II) the Congressman wrote that the American people were embarrassed by such a denial of a visa to *"a distinguished literary and political figure"* such as Marquez. In justifying his sponsorship of the Frank amendment, he wrote, *"America was frequently embarrassed"* by the *"exclusion of foreigners whose political views various Americans found objectionable."*

The McCarran-Walter Act was a cold war era law that excluded members or affiliates of "subversive groups" from obtaining visas. The term subversive was a common euphemism for Communist. Putting aside the snide swipe by Frank at those of us who might still harbor objections to a friend of the bloody handed tyrant Castro visiting this country and making satchels full of money selling books to gullible elitist Ivy League college students, Marquez posed only as a threat to the trust funds of those who would be inclined to consider his ilk to be a "distinguished literary and political figure."

One could reasonably argue that Marquez and other basically harmless intellectual left-wing totalitarians no longer threaten American national security. As a member of Congress, Barney Frank could have simply filed a resolution in the House sponsoring a visit to the United States for private citizen Gabriel Garcia Marquez.

In fact, most of these so-called left-wing intellectuals would've no doubt found a member of Congress willing to sponsor a visit. The beauty of this approach would be that the sponsoring Congressman, by implication, would be held directly and personally responsible for the actions and the behavior of the guest who was helped with the special invitation. The President, on advise of the Attorney General, would retain the right to veto the invitation on the grounds that such an invitation would either contradict American foreign policy or pose as a national security threat.

Instead of taking this simple constitutional and logical approach to the problem, an approach that carried responsibility, accountability, and political risk, Frank instead chose to apply the method of sponsoring a heavy handed and sweeping new law. The Frank amendment essentially gutted the McCarran-Walter Act. Henceforth, almost anyone with a political agenda but not proven to have been involved with "terrorist activities" would be able to enter the country on a legal visa. The questionable applicant would henceforth be welcomed into the country with no sponsor and no accountability to anyone.

The Frank amendment includes language that purports to preserve the right of the government to deny entry to an applicant known to be involved with "terrorist activity." Such a right had already existed in law going back to 1798 and the passage of the Alien Enemies act signed by President John Adams. What the Frank amendment specifically changed, besides narrowing the definition of what would constitute terrorist activities, was that the government would no longer be legally allowed to deny a visa using the stated politics or ideology of the applicant as evidence of ill intent. The amendment specifically *"Repeals the ideological grounds for exclusion."*

The Frank amendment was effective, thought astonishingly misguided, in hampering the government's ability to deny visas to anyone based upon their political orientation. The Congressman was motivated by a stated desire to help left-wing intellectuals with whom he seemed to feel an affinity as evidenced by the aforementioned essay. Yet the actual if unintended effect of the amendment was that people affiliated with groups such as Hamas along with the nineteen al

Queda affiliated September 11 hijackers and countless others who meant to do grave harm to this country would be the beneficiaries of the new law.

None of those affiliated with Hamas or the 9/11 hijackers who entered this country legally after the Frank amendment went into effect were formally affiliated with "terrorist activities" by the new and more narrow definition of that term. The influx of terrorists accelerated in the 1990's, according to the acclaimed filmmaker and author Steven Emerson, who studied the phenomena for many years and who is regarded as a leading expert on Islamic terrorism in America. Emerson is the creator of the award-winning documentary "Jihad in America."

Emerson, testifying before the Senate Judiciary Committee's Subcommittee on Terrorism, Technology, and Government Information on February 24, 1998, described the domestic threat. He testified that American based *"radical Islamic groups such as the Council on American Islamic Relations (CAIR) and the American Muslim Council (AMC)...have defended terrorist groups, terrorist leaders including Hamas chieftain Musa Marzook and World Trade Center bombing conspiracy ringleader Sheik Omar Abdul Rahman, and the Sudanese terrorist regime currently engaged in a genocidal war against the Christian minority."* (7.) These groups are alleged to be associated with "charities" which stand accused of funneling money to terrorists overseas.

Emerson testified *"Both of these groups have sponsored visits in the United States of leading international militants and known anti-Semites (including those who exhorted their followers to kill Jews) and consistently attacked American writers for exposing the threat of militant Islamic extremism."* (8.) The visitors apparently had no problem obtaining visas and proceeded to spew anti American and anti Semitic propaganda while raising money, recruiting followers, and intimidating critics including the vast majority of moderate American Muslims. While here, they enjoyed all the benefits and constitutional rights enjoyed by American citizens.

Emerson testified that the first World Trade Center attack, instigated by the blind Sheik Omar Abdul Rahman, who had obtained his visa in 1990, one year after the Frank amendment went into effect along with the dismantling of the ABCC, was followed by the discovery of an Islamic extremist terror infrastructure in the United States. Intelligence officials and law enforcement would uncover in the next 5 years a massive and loosely affiliated terror network. Emerson told the subcommittee *"These groups have created large networks of supporters from whom they have raised tens of millions of dollars for their movements, recruited and trained new followers, underwritten their brethren organizations in the Middle East and elsewhere, and even remotely directed terrorist operations back in the Middle East or Europe."*(9.) Emerson himself was warned by the FBI that there was a hit squad looking for him soon after the release of his documentary "Jihad in America."

Oliver Revell, former Associate Deputy Director of the FBI, testified that *"the United States is the most preferred and easiest place in the world for radical Islamic groups to set up their headquarters to wage war in their homelands, destabilize and attack American allies and ultimately move against the United States itself."*(10.) Emerson testified that *"living in the West and in particular the United States has provided militant Islamic groups with freedoms and maneuverability like they never experienced in their native lands. Freedom to disseminate extremist propaganda calling for death and violence; to raise an almost unlimited amount of funds for their organizations; to remotely direct terrorist operations back in their host countries; and to exploit the other freedoms of American society."*(11.)

In his testimony, Emerson recounted two examples of how terrorists, visiting on Frank amendment visas, were helped by what he described as the "militant Islamic infrastructure in the United States." Ali Abu Kamal, a Palestinian visiting from Gaza, pulled a gun on the tourist deck of the Empire State Building in Manhattan and before committing suicide, killed one young man and permanently wounded another, rendering him brain damaged for the rest of his life. Emerson testified that law enforcement officials found out that Abu Kamal had received assistance by members of a Florida mosque who helped him get a gun, accompanied him on target practice and escorted him on a planned but aborted assassination attempt in Miami. Emerson also testified that two militant Palestinians were arrested in New York hours before their crudely made bombs were set to be detonated in the New York City subway system. Had the attack had gone off as planned, and not been thwarted by an informant, possibly thousands could have been killed. (12.)

The Frank amendment raised the bar and made it more difficult for government officials to prove a connection between the visa applicant and terrorist activities. Mere association with a group deemed to be espousing terrorism would no longer be enough to deny a visa. Frank himself addressed the issue in "Barney

Frank's Views on the Terrorism Bill", written as a criticism of post 9/11 anti-terrorism legislation when hw wrote *"The bill would have allowed the exclusion of visa applicants who had 'endorsed or espoused terrorist activity'…but the mere 'espousal or endorsement' of terrorist activity casts far too wide a net of exclusion."*

It should be reiterated that Frank fought for this legislation at a time when terrorists were already a proven threat to America and had already demonstrated their willingness to ruthlessly kill American citizens both here and around the world. It is unprecedented in international law and custom for any sovereign state, today or in history, to be hamstrung in such a manner.

In "Barney Frank's Views on the Terrorism Bill, written after 9/11, the Congressman defends his amendment with the incredulous rationalization that since American citizens have the right to free speech and free expression, those same rights ought to be extended to foreigners who want to come here to express themselves because our right to free expression is somehow *"impinged when we exclude people because we find their political views unpopular, unsettling, or dangerous."*

The Congressman's insists that the *"espousal or endorsement of terrorist activity casts too wide a net of exclusion."* Really? Consider the case of Sami al-Arian, the alleged leader of Islamic Jihad, an organization which claimed responsibility for the 1995 murder of Alisa Flatow, an American citizen, in a Gaza Strip terrorist attack.

Al-Arian had no problem obtaining a visa to teach at the University of Florida in the 1990's. It would've been difficult for the government to prove that al-Arian was engaged in terrorist activities even though he was caught on video delivering a speech in Chicago where he was clearly engaging in the "espousal or endorsement of terrorist activity." Had it not been for the Frank amendment, and had President Reagan's ABCC been left in place to do its job, Sami al-Arian, a non-citizen, and other advocates of terrorism would have been more easily detained and deported.

Frank has written that decisions made by immigration officials regarding the denial of visas ought to undergo judicial review. This aspect of the legislation filed by the Congressman, requiring that both government officials and American embassy officials be subject to judicial review when denying a visa has made it more difficult for our elected officials and their appointed representatives to deny visas. The Constitution does not grant the judicial branch of government the power to review visa applications. In fact, the setting of immigration policy has traditionally resided with the executive and the legislature.

The President has traditionally retained the prerogative to set visa policy under the same principle that gives the President the power to set foreign or diplomatic policy. Visiting this country is a privilege, not a constitutional right. The policy of setting up a system of judicial review for applicants sets up another hoop immigration officials and embassies have to jump through before denying a visa to someone who, in their judgment, should not be let in.

Frank contends that without judicial review, immigration officials, acting according to directives from the executive, might be able to exclude "supporters of the African National Congress or the Irish Republican Army." But why shouldn't our elected leaders decide whether any member of any group, for whatever reason, should be granted the right to visit this country? Decisions regarding the issuance of visas ought to reside with officials elected to represent the interests and aspirations of those who elect them. This is the constitutional and democratic approach.

Until the Frank amendment, no government in history was ever legally required to admit any person or group that the government chose not to admit for any reason. John Adams Alien Act of 1798 had protected this country in this regard for almost two hundred years. Adams law, a version of which is in place within the laws of every sovereign nation in existence today and in history, is an expression of one of the most basic functions of national sovereignty.

As individuals, we exercise the maximum amount of latitude when deciding who is invited into our homes. There are property laws that protect this right. Nations have the same natural right. Indeed nations are charged with a practical and a moral responsibility to exercise that right in order to protect the national home. Any attempt to try to subvert those rights is wrong and is a recipe for catastrophe as we have seen.

Frank does not think that the government should have the right to deny visas to those deemed to be terrorists for political reasons. In other words, to Frank's way of thinking, it isn't enough for a person to espouse or advocate terrorism or violence, a person must be proven to have engaged in terrorist activity or violence to be denied a visa. To make his argument he complains in the article that Nelson

Mandela and Gerry Adams were excluded from entering the country because they were declared to be terrorists by the government.

He points out that the Clinton Administration was nevertheless able to exclude Gerry Adams even after the passage of his amendment as proof that the government was still able to deny entry even with his amendment in place but this entirely misses the point. In a specific case, the President or the Attorney General could override the Frank amendment and deny a visa to a specific person but what about the thousands of everyday applicants who might be entering in order to form sleeper cells? Gerry Adams was the exception to the rule.

Frank states in the article that he was concerned that the "endorsed or espoused" part of his amendment, if removed by the USA Patriot Act *"could lead to a renewal of some restrictions on people whom Americans should continue to have a right to hear if they so choose."* Since when does the right of Americans to hear whatever they choose to hear mean that an expositor of those views, a foreigner who might be at least indirectly fomenting violence or engaging in subversive activity, have a right to come here and to express those views?

Using this twisted logic, hatemongering neo-Nazis or ideological supporters of Osama bin Laden, not formally connected to "terrorist activities," would have the right to visit this country, get their followers to rent out halls and promote their appearances, and then give speeches spewing hatred and racism. Unfortunately, this is exactly what happened with the arrival of the Jihadists after the Frank amendment became law.

According to Steven Emerson, followers of the ideology of Hamas started visiting this country on Frank amendment visas to deliver hate filled speeches to jam-packed Mosques and halls in urban predominantly Muslim neighborhoods. These events, according to Gerald Posner, were used by the terrorists to scout out new recruits.

Our INS and overseas embassies were turned into revolving turnstiles for those advocating views that were "unpopular, unsettling, or dangerous" to quote from Frank's article. A nation must at all times, and as a basic article of survival, retain the right to exclude those foreigners who seek to enter this country for the purpose of espousing and fomenting violence, religious intolerance, and ethnic hatred.

Several times during our debates and on the Boston TV show Newsnight with Chet Curtis and Jim Braude on New England Cable News, Barney Frank, in response to my accusation about the 9/11 terrorists, stated flatly that the 9/11 hijackers were here illegally. That assertion was flat out false in every case but two and in those two cases, the visa had expired a few months before the hijacking.

Paul Mulshine of the Star Ledger quoted from a letter written to him from Frank in response to his column regarding the legality of the visa's of the 9/11 terrorists. Frank stated "Every one of the terrorists involved in Sept. 11 was completely excludable under this law."

Sure, the terrorists were excludable if the full extent of their background had been known. The officials weren't allowed to consider political opinion or depend upon a hunch in denying a visa, which seriously hampered the possibility that an investigation would be started. By the late 1990's, government officials had become so used to looking the other way on issues such as the politics of the applicant, and so used to suppressing thoughts about the overall appearance of the applicant, that the ability and desire to make judgments had long been drummed out of the picture. After all, the worst possible situation an official could find himself in, a situation that could result in his dismissal, the besmirching of his reputation, and even criminal charges brought against him, would be to be accused of being a bigot.

To be denied a visa, the terrorist would literally have to admit he was a terrorist. For example, the 9/11 Commission report shows an illustration of the visa application of hijacker Mahwan al Shehi. Next to Shehi's hate-filled face are the words, "Are you a member or a representative of a terrorist organization?" Al Shehi checked the "no" box. His application for a visa was approved without further question.

If the ABCC had been left in place to do its job back in the 1980's, those hijackers would never have gotten into this country at all, or if they had, the government would have had a running chance of detaining and expelling them. If our officials charged with the responsibility of granting visas had been left to do their jobs without Frank's utopian meddling, our government would have had the tools to stop them before they had the chance to commit the worst single terrorist act of mass murder in American history.

A Date, which will live in Infamy

On the morning of Tuesday, September 11, 2001 my wife and I were driving our three-year-old daughter to her first day of nursery school. I was already painfully aware, as a Jew, of the increase in terrorism against Jews in Israel that year. Israel had been convulsed with murderous suicide bombers who were routinely blowing up busloads of Israeli men, women and children and blowing themselves up in crowds in order to kill as many Jews as possible.

A mixture of an acute awareness of what was going on in Israel and a natural anxiety over my only child's first day at school, located on the first floor of an urban synagogue, filled me with a sense of dread that day. On the Monday before 9/11, I sat with other parents whose children would be starting school the next day for orientation. Listening to the presentation, I found myself fixing my attention on the massive glass picture window located behind the instructor's head and facing into my daughter's pre-school classroom at street level. I found myself conjuring up an image in my imagination of an Arab terrorist dressed in fatigues and a white-checkered headscarf wielding a machine gun and breaking through the glass. The mood that day was tense and grim.

I had to get to work that Tuesday morning so after I dropped my wife and daughter off at the school, with my wife staying behind with the other mothers to help the toddlers get adjusted, I hit the road. As I drove toward downtown the news broke over the radio that a plane had crashed into the World Trade Center in New York. In the half hour that followed, rumors flew like lightening across the airwaves including a report that a car bomb had exploded outside the State Department and that a bomber was heading for the White House and the Capitol Building. It seemed to me, and I would imagine to most people listening to the radio at that moment, like the government itself was being overthrown and that we were in a total state of war.

I turned the car around and hightailed it back to the school to get my wife and daughter out of there. By the time I parked the car and ran into the building, I was so out of breath that I could barely talk. I struggled to regain my composure and proceeded to inform the unwitting mothers, through gasps, what was going on. Everyone proceeded to solemnly but quickly fetch their children and head home. I and most everyone else in America and around the world spent the rest of the day glued to the TV watching the devastation as it unfolded in New York and Washington.

I wrote a column later that day and sent it to various opinion websites. The theme was the speech that had been delivered by President Franklin Delano Roosevelt to a joint session of Congress on December 8th following the 1941 Japanese attack on Pearl Harbor. Those resolute remarks at that dark hour are republished here in full:

December 8, 1941

Yesterday, December 7, 1941—a date which will live in infamy—the United States of America was suddenly and deliberately attacked by naval and air forces of the Empire of Japan.

The United States was at peace with that nation and, at the solicitation of Japan, was still in conversation with its Government and its Emperor looking toward the maintenance of peace in the Pacific. Indeed, one hour after Japanese air squadrons had commenced bombing in Oahu, the Japanese Ambassador to the United States and his colleague delivered to the Secretary of State a formal reply to a recent American message. While this reply stated that it seemed useless to continue the existing diplomatic negotiations, it contained no threat or hint of war or armed attack.

It will be recorded that the distance of Hawaii from Japan makes it obvious that the attack was deliberately planned many days or even weeks ago. During the intervening time the Japanese Government has deliberately sought to deceive the United States by false statements and expressions of hope for continued peace.

The attack yesterday on the Hawaiian Islands has caused severe damage to American naval and military forces. Very many American lives have been lost. In addition American ships have been reported torpedoed on the high seas between San Francisco and Honolulu.

Yesterday the Japanese Government also launched an attack against Malaya. Last night Japanese forces attacked Hong Kong. Last night Japanese forces attacked Guam. Last night Japanese forces attacked the Philippine Islands. Last night the Japanese attacked Wake Island. This morning the Japanese attacked Midway Island.

Japan has, therefore, undertaken a surprise offensive extending throughout the Pacific area. The facts of yesterday speak for themselves. The people of the United States have already formed their opinions and well understand the implications to the very life and safety of our nation.

As Commander-in-Chief of the Army and Navy, I have directed that all measures be taken for our defense.

Always will we remember the character of the onslaught against us. No matter how long it may take us to overcome this premeditated invasion, the American people in their righteous might will win through to absolute victory.

I believe I interpret the will of the Congress and of the people when I assert that we will not only defend ourselves to the uttermost but will make very certain that this form of treachery shall never endanger us again.

Hostilities exist. There is no blinking at the fact that our people, our territory and our interests are in grave danger.

With confidence in our armed forces—with the unbounded determination of our people—we will gain the inevitable triumph—so help us God.

I ask that the Congress declare that since the unprovoked and dastardly attack by Japan on Sunday, December seventh, a state of war has existed between the United States and the Japanese Empire."

In the summer following the 9/11 attacks, my daughter attended a day camp, which was held in a small park adjacent to the synagogue where she had attended nursery school. The synagogue had invested in security locks and punch codes and there was heightened protection from local police. The parents decided to organize a daily watch over the children with the volunteering parent sitting near the entrance of the park holding a cell phone and watching for strangers. I volunteered on Mondays.

Israeli parents and grandparents had been regularly watching over nursery schools since the 1974 Maalot attack. On May 5, 1974, ultra-leftist terrorists of the PDFLP, an offshoot of the PLO, had invaded a school in the Northern Israeli town of Maalot holding children hostage for 3 days. The terrorists eventually sprayed the room with machine gun fire killing 22 children and 5 adults and wounding 56. The difference between the Israeli bubbas and zaydas standing guard over their children in Israel and me is that they hold guns and they know how to use them.

Twelve years later, in 1986, eight members of the PFLP, another leftist offshoot of the PLO, were arrested in Los Angeles. Congressman Frank reacted by submitting the Frank amendment to Congress, which led to the disbanding of the ABCC, the organization responsible for those arrests. The Congressman apparently felt that it was wrong for the government to detain members of the PFLP on mere suspicion. The PFLP members were non-citizens here on visas. While the FBI had no proof that these eight men were involved in "terrorist activities," it was nevertheless determined that these visitors were involved in fundraising for "charities" and propagandizing for terrorist groups.

Even after 9/11 the Congressman continues to champion the cause of suspected terrorists here on visas made possible largely as a result of his many legislative initiatives. The Congressman expressed outrage over the detention of suspected non-citizens by the Justice Department in the wake of 9/11 and the conditions of their detention at Camp X Ray at Guantanamo Bay, Cuba.

In June of 2003 I attended a speech delivered by Congressman Frank at my synagogue, the same synagogue that had tightened security. In that speech, Barney Frank spoke of his attempt to free an American citizen who had been detained in Communist China. This man, while visiting China, had been detained by the Chinese authorities on suspicion of spying.

The Congressman told his audience that he had contacted the Chinese government in an effort to obtain this citizens release. The Chinese responded to his entreaty with the assertion that the United States was in no position to lecture them about freeing anyone given the fact that America was detaining people at camp x ray. He proceeded to draw a moral equivalence between the American government detention of suspected foreign terrorists after 9/11 and that of the bloody handed Communist dictatorship when he asserted that he agreed with the Chinese position. He then went on to attack Attorney General John Ashcroft, whom he compared to the Chinese dictator.

The Aftermath

In May of 2002, the Department of Justice Office of the Inspector General released the 188-page report known as The 9/11 Commission Report—Final Report of the National Commission on Terrorist Attacks Upon the United States. The 9/11 commission examined many events leading up to the 9/11 attack including the fact that the Immigration and Naturalization Service had mailed forms notifying the Florida flight school of a change in the visa status of the two of the September 11 terrorists, Mohamed Atta and Marwan al-Shehhi. Both had trained as pilots at the flight school. (1.)

The flight school received the forms approving a change in their immigration status from "visitor" to "student" six months after the terrorists had committed suicide while blowing up the twin towers and Pentagon. The amazing and chilling aspect of this revelation was the ease in which the INS had changed the visa status of the terrorists. This symbolizes, both literally and metaphorically, how bad things had gotten with regard to the issuance of visas.

Scrutiny of foreign students had already long gone by the wayside thanks to Congressman Frank and his "reform" which loosened standards for admitting and monitoring foreign students. The FBI, CIA, and other agencies had forgotten how to exchange information and how to coordinate efforts long ago thanks to the Frank amendment and the subsequent disbanding of the ABCC. Immigrations officials had long ago learned to avert their attention from considering the applicant's political beliefs as a cause for investigation or denial of a visa. In the 1990's, terrorists were thumbing their noses and operating out in the open and under the color of the law while government agencies and officials were worried about being accused of racial profiling.

The 9/11 commission also examined how both Atta and al-Shehi were admitted into the United States on three separate occasions in 2000 and 2001 which tells us everything we need to know about the state of the monitoring and tracking of visa applicants. The teacher and student visa program sponsored by the

Congressman had made no provision for the monitoring of students to ensure that they were in school. Several of the 9/11 hijackers were holders of student visas. Besides Atta and al-Shehhi, Flight 77 hijacker Hani Hanjour also held a student visa. Hanjour never actually attended a school. Hijackers Atta and al-Shehi knew that laws governing student visas were more liberal which was why they switched from visitor status.

The 9/11 commission indicated that as of June 2002, the INS had estimated that approximately 355,000 nondetained aliens with final removal orders had failed to leave the country as required. Government agencies had long ago stopped coordinating investigations into aliens with expired visas thanks to the defanging of the ABCC. Several of the 9/11 hijackers held expired visas on the morning they boarder those passenger planes armed with box cutters.

With regard to Atta and al-Shehhi's entries into the United States, according to the 9/11 commission, evidence did not show that the INS inspectors who admitted them violated INS policies and practices. Atta and al-Shehhi had each entered the United States three times at separate airports. They had valid passports and visitor visas, according to the 9/11 Commission, and their visas were good for multiple entries.

Atta and al-Shehhi were admitted into the country because, according to the 9/11 commission, the INS inspectors lacked important information when assessing their eligibility for admission into the United States. The 9/11 commission investigators were consistently told by INS inspectors at the ports of entry (POEs) they visited that "aliens who intended to enter the United States to become full-time students and who lacked the required student visas likely would have been admitted through a waiver process."

Regarding the terrorist hijackers, the "9-11 Commission Report" states (p. 237):

> The muscle hijackers began arriving in the United States in late April 2001. In most cases they traveled in pairs on tourist visas and entered the United States in Orlando or Miami, Florida; Washington D.C.; or New York. Atta and Shehhi assisted those arriving in Florida, while Hazmi and Hanjour took care of the rest. By the end of June, 14 of the 15 muscle hijackers had crossed the Atlantic.

The September 11 terrorist ringleaders included:

Mohamed Atta, leader of the hijackers, who landed in Newark, N.J., from Prague on a visitor's visa issued in Berlin on June 3, 1999. He crashed American Airlines Flight 11 into the South Tower of the World Trade Center;

Ziad al-Jarrah, the pilot of United Airlines Flight 93, which crashed in Pennsylvania. He received his pilot's license in Hamburg, Germany, and entered the United States on June 27 at Newark;

Marwan al Shehhi, pilot of United Airlines Flight 175, which crashed into the North Tower. He arrived in the United States at Newark on May 29, 2000, on a tourist visa issued in the United Arab Emirates, and cleared customs in less than a half-hour;

Hani Honjour, pilot of American Airlines Flight 77, which crashed into the Pentagon. He first entered the United States on a student visa in 1996, returned to Saudi Arabia, then traveled from the United Arab Emirates back to the United States in December 2000 on a student visa.

The Developing Story

Tom Mountain writes for the Newton Tab. Barney Frank's hometown newspaper serves the predominantly liberal Boston suburb of Newton, Massachusetts. Mountain interviewed me for an upcoming column which would be published under the heading "Barney Frank's role in 9/11" on April 13, 2005. Mountain's column on the Frank immigration legislation is one of the best I've read on the topic and its publication set off a chain of events that would come to include the publication of this book.

Frank shot back at Mountain the next week with "Mountain Lies (Tab 4/20)." The crux of the defense of the Frank amendment, further illustrated in a letter by Frank to the editor "Morse, Posner are still wrong"(Tab 5/4) which was written in response to my published letter "Give Rep. Frank a Fair Hearing (Tab 4/27) was his insistence that Gerald Posner's comment from Why America Slept "a visa could only be denied if the government could prove that the applicant had committed an act of terrorism" is wrong.

To illustrate the point, Frank quotes from his own legislation, the Frank amendment itself with the following: "Any alien who (I) has engaged in a terrorist activity, or (II) a consular officer or the Attorney General knows, or has reasonable ground to believe, is likely to engage after entry in any terrorist activity (as defined in clause (iii)), is excludable."

In commenting on the portion of the legislation he quoted, Frank goes on to write: "The government does not have to "prove" anything; it has to have a "reasonable ground to believe" that there would be a problem." His claim that Posner was wrong is actually a re-iteration that Posner was right. Posner was not quoting from the bill itself, he was writing about the consequences of the bill, which was that, in fact, the government would henceforth have to prove that the visa applicant had a link to terrorism before denying a visa. That is exactly what "reasonable ground to believe" means. Frank is parsing words and is furiously trying to spin his way out of responsibility.

Frank further comments: "What the government has to have reason to believe is not that the applicant had committed an act of terrorism, but only that he or she was likely to commit such an act in the future." Again, "reason to believe" is another way of saying proof and that is exactly how the law was supposed to be enforced.

As he did during the campaign, Frank, in his letter, hides behind the alleged fig leaf of his so-called absolvement of guilt, which he defensively claims was offered by Tom Keane, the co-chairman of the 9/11 Commission. One of the flaws of the Commission report is that it was careful to not affix blame on anyone and, in fact, worked to avoid naming anyone of either party so as to avoid getting into a partisan squabble. This aspect of the report was a dis-service since it leaves that important aspect of the investigation to others.

As he also did during the campaign, Frank, in his letter, hides behind the coat tails of others who signed the bill putting aside the fact that he was the chief sponsor and the bill is called the Frank Amendment. Of course, this tactic wouldn't be necessary if Frank was sure the bill was right.

He ends the letter by questioning my motivation for pursuing the issue, which he implies, has to do with my conservative politics. In doing so, he insults the intelligence of his own liberal base since security from terrorism is hardly a partisan issue. He is, by implication, suggesting that the weakening of standards regarding the granting of visas to potential terrorists is a liberal cause. I would hope that fair-minded liberals would reject such a notion.

When I first started discussing the Frank amendment and its consequences with voters I met during my 2004 campaign for Congress in Massachusetts, the reaction on the street was often based not upon common sense but rather upon the ideological orientation of the listener. Most people were simply not prepared to think negatively about the well-entrenched Congressman and the topic was too terrible to get their minds around. After all, several of the hijackers stayed overnight in Newton and had taken off from Logan Airport in Boston, before hijacking the passenger jets and turning them into self-guided missiles.

Starting out, I had naively assumed that an issue of this nature would cut across ideological lines. After all, I reasoned, liberals were just as angry as conservatives to discover that the 9/11 terrorists had been in this country legally and had been operating with virtual impunity right under our noses and the nose of our government. There were, after all, at least as many liberals as conservatives boarding those passenger jets on that fateful morning. There was no doubt as many liberals as conservatives sitting at their desks, logging on to their computers, chatting with their co-workers, and glancing at pictures of their families resting lovingly on their desks at the World Trade Center and at the Pentagon when planes exploded through the walls.

I quickly and sadly came to observe the reaction of many liberals to this issue and that reaction was a knee jerk defense of the indefensible. Many of the liberals I spoke with, certainly the true believer types, were more concerned that the Frank amendment might expose the darker side of their own reverently held political beliefs than they were with ascertaining the truth. The irrational reaction was perhaps based on an underlying concern that the Frank amendment could expose the colossal failure of other so called liberal initiatives when put into practice in the real world.

The disastrous and perhaps the inevitable result of the Frank amendment called into question other false and utopian ideas that had also been codified into law over the years. Exposure of the fallacy of the Frank Amendment threatened "progress" and could "turn the clock back" on certain definitions of progress. Many other policies pushed by liberals had also failed over the years and had also hurt people although not quite as dramatically as the Frank amendment had. There was a noticeable circling of the wagons.

In his advocacy of this legislation, I would speculate that Frank was motivated by a core belief that absolute and de-facto equality can be legislated not just for Americans but for everyone in the world. The aspect of that belief that separates the Frank amendment from similar and less grandiose domestic initiatives is an ambitious attempt to legislate absolute equality to the entire world by legally declaring that visitation to the United States was an absolute right. For our government to deny this so-called right, unless there is a high standard of proof that the visitor intended to carry out a harmful physical act against Americans based upon past provable activity, would constitute an act of discrimination in Frank's crazy-quilt view.

The Frank amendment denied our law enforcement officials charged with the responsibility of protecting the lives and property of American citizens, the ability to make reasonable and informed judgments with regard to the issuing of visas to foreign applicants. This came to include FBI agents, CIA operatives, INS officials, embassy officials, and State and Justice Department officials.

Congressman Frank was concerned that, in denying a visa, an official might be influenced by a personal agenda or by bigotry so he created legislation that would end that possibility by taking away the right to decide. With the threat of terrorism well known at the time the Frank amendment was passed into law, dabbling in utopian agendas was playing Russian roulette with American lives and we have tragically reaped the bitter harvest.

Frank's contempt for American intelligence agencies knows no bounds. During our debates, he sarcastically answered with the assertion that his advocacy of the CIA budget cut was because the Soviet Union was dead, in case I hadn't noticed, and therefore the CIA presence should've been scaled back in Russia. The Frank cuts to the CIA, which were passed into law in 1997, occurred after there had been a considerable ratcheting up of terrorist acts against Americans both domestically and around the world. Two examples out of many that could be cited are the first World Trade Center bombing, which occurred in 1993, and the Khobar Tower bombing which had occurred in Saudi Arabia in 1995.

Author David Horowitz touched upon the issue of the CIA budget cut in his pamphlet "How the Left Undermined America's Security":

"In 1995, 1996 and 1997, Barney Frank introduced a similar amendment (to one offered by Bernie Sanders) that would have cut intelligence funds by less, but cut them still. In 1997, 158 Democrats voted for the Frank amendment. The same year, a majority voted for a modified Sanders amendment that cut intelligence funding by five per cent."

On December 4, 1998, following the terrorist bombing of the American embassies in Nairobi and Dar es Salaam, President Bill Clinton's CIA Director George Tenet issued the following directive to several CIA officials: *"We are at war. I want no resources or people spared in this effort, either inside CIA or the Community."* (3.)

The main threat to peace and security today is radical Islam, as we have all been so painfully been made aware. During the campaign, I discussed how Frank's involvement in immigration matters had weakened America's hand in the war against Islamic terrorism and had put every American at risk. Frank preferred to discuss old wars that had already been won during times when America knew how to put American interests first.

After the collapse of the Soviet Union in 1990, the Communist threat to the free world was largely supplanted by the threat of radical Islam. Communism and Nazism historically have a lot in common with the radical Islamic movement of today. They all share a totalitarian belief in the necessity of world domination, they possess the insane view that the force of arms is a redemptive vehicle to achieve that end, and they view the western democracies, particularly the "great Satan" America, as the primary obstacle blocking the path to their bizarre concept of an enlightened utopia.

There are essential differences however between those historic movements, which reached their respective apex in Adolf Hitler's Germany, Josef Stalin's Russia and Mao tse Tung's China, and today's radical Islamist movement of Osama bin Laden. The Nazis were popular in parts of Europe and the third world and the Communists found many converts and sympathizers amongst elitist circles primarily in the western democracies and in America.

The radical Islamists, on the other hand, have no significant following outside the Muslim sphere. They have little influence in America, which is why they are dependent on outsiders coming into the country to perform vicious acts of terrorism. The Frank amendment was intended to help those so-called intellectuals who still clung to the old and false doctrines of Communism. While Frank wanted to help these dinosaurs make their way on to American campuses to sing their paeans to elitist college students, instead the laws the Congressman pushed through Congress swung open the door to the radical Jihadists.

America maintained an uneasy balance of power over several decades with the Soviet Union, in a policy that was known as MAD, mutual assured destruction. No such restraint exists today with the radical Islamists. They have proven to be capable of blowing themselves to smithereens on their way to paradise in order to kill as many "infidels" as possible. The difference between the two, and the threat the radical Jihadists pose, must have been known to Barney Frank at the time the

Frank amendment was passed into law. It was certainly understood instinctively by the rest of us.

Gerald Posner, whose book "Why America Slept" first brought the issue of the Frank amendment to my attention as well as to the attention of countless Americans who read the New York Times bestseller, granted an interview to Jim Hand, a reporter with the Attleboro Sun Chronicle. In the Hand article "Congress candidates swap claims—Frank says Morse accusations on terror law a lie (4/22/04)" Posner told the reporter that he wrote about the Frank amendment to *show "the different mindset the country and the government had prior to Sept. 11, 2001…That tells you where the country was prior to 9/11"* Posner said in describing the Frank amendment.

With all due respect to Mr. Posner, this view is all too typical and completely misses the point of why America in fact did sleep. Of course the country had a different mindset back then. That was a time when our government still operated in the best national interest. That was before the government was put to sleep by the Frank amendment and terrorists began crowding our shores. That was before foreign racists and anti-Semites began entering with Frank amendment visas, stirring up hatred, and raising funds through "charities" for terrorism overseas.

That was before America felt the full destructive impact of the Frank amendment. Times didn't just change as if by magic. Bad ideas, when put into practice, really do reap consequences.

APPENDIX A

Mountain: Barney Frank's role in 9/11
By **Tom Mountain—Newton Tab**
Wednesday, April 13, 2005

Gerald Posner, author of "Case Closed," the widely acclaimed book on the assassination of President Kennedy, has penned another blockbuster, "Why America Slept—The Failure to Prevent 9/11." In it, Posner details how over two decades the breakdown in authority, jurisdiction and communication among the various levels of the government responsible for protecting our borders and preventing terrorist infiltration led directly to the establishment of foreign terrorist sleeper cells in the United States, which culminated in the terrorist bombings of Sept. 11, 2001.

What Posner reveals is nothing short of startling, as he details the misguided complicity of none other than our own Congressman Barney Frank, whose meddling in the immigration laws since the early 1980s had disastrous consequences:

"Congressman Barney Frank, the Massachusetts Democrat who was a strong advocate of protecting civil liberties, led a successful effort to amend the Immigration and Nationality Act so that membership in a terrorist group was no longer sufficient to deny a visa.

"Under Frank's amendment, which seems unthinkable post 9/11, a visa could only be denied if the government could prove that the applicant had committed an act of terrorism. Rendered toothless by the Frank amendment, the Reagan administration had virtually no way to block entry visas even when there was information linking the individuals to terrorist groups."

And so it began.

Since 1798, when President John Adams signed into law the Alien Enemies Act, the country had legally and effectively prevented known or suspected enemy agents or terrorists from gaining entry into the United States. But the various amendments to the immigration laws put forth by Barney Frank over the span of two decades derailed this crucial government policy, which had worked remarkably well for nearly two centuries.

Between 1981 and 2001, Barney Frank sponsored no less than 13 amendments to the Immigration and Nationality Act, which had the effect of opening the nation's floodgates to a well-disciplined, well-organized network of terrorist sleeper cells and support groups that have since become entrenched here in America for up to two decades.

The Frank Amendment of 1989, the crown jewel of the congressman's assault on our immigration laws, declared that a foreigner could not be denied a visa because of his ideology, which meant that no matter how repugnant, hostile or undemocratic an individual's politics, those could not be grounds for denying him entry into the United States.

What's more, the very essence of what constituted terrorist activities was redefined by Frank, as his 2004 political opponent and talk show host Chuck Morse explains, "The Frank Amendment raised the bar and made it more difficult for government officials to prove a connection between the visa applicant and terrorist activities. Mere association with a group deemed to be involved with terrorism would no longer be enough to deny a visa as it had been previously."

Morse continues, "None of those affiliated with Hamas or the 9/11 hijackers who entered the country legally after the Frank Amendment went into effect were formally affiliated with 'terrorist activities' by the new and more narrow definition of the term.

Yet the Frank Amendment of 1989 was hardly alone in damaging the national interest. As early as 1981, Frank sponsored an amendment to greatly expand the teacher and student visa program. The new definition for each was so vague and diluted, and the means for verifying that these special visa recipients were actually enrolled as students or teachers was so unenforceable, that the 9/11 terrorist commander Mohammed Atta obtained a student visa knowing that immigration authorities would never check up on him. And he was correct.

In 1995, after Brandeis student Alisa Flatow was murdered by Islamic Jihad in the Gaza Strip, it was revealed that Sami al-Arian, the alleged leader of Islamic Jihad, had easily obtained a teaching visa to the University of Florida, made possible by H.R. Amendment 5287, sponsored by Congressman Frank.

The Frank Amendment opened the doors to our nation for some of the most unseemly characters ever to come out of the Middle East. Aside from the unprecedented influx of foreign terrorists, a large support group of foreign anti-American radical Muslim sympathizers sprouted up in the 1990s as a result of these new lax visa requirements. This was even further exacerbated by follow up legislation from Frank, which effectively tied the hands of overseas American consular officials by stripping them of their traditional discretion in granting visas, then impeding the CIA and FBI from even sharing information about these questionable aliens once they landed in America.

So having sabotaged those immigration laws which had succeeded in keeping out foreign terrorists for nearly two centuries, Frank then proceeded to launch a campaign against CIA funding during the Clinton administration, which resulted in severe CIA budget cuts in 1996, despite the warnings from Clinton's CIA director, George Tenet, of an ominous terrorist threat.

In my conversation with Mr. Frank, he referred to Posner's book (soon to be made into a TV miniseries) as "a shockingly bad book." He then railed against his political nemesis Chuck Morse as "delusional" and predictably blamed the Republicans, whom he contends, "rewrote the immigration laws in 1995."

The Congressman exhibited an almost exasperated disbelief when I continued to query him, as if I were a knave to even dare to question his legislative record. When I evidently let on that I was less than convinced by his response, he questioned whether I had listened to anything he had already told me. So chagrined was Mr. Frank that someone should be disinclined to accept his rhetoric as gospel.

It also struck me that not since Boston Herald columnist Howie Carr raked him over the coals during the infamous male prostitute scandal had any member of the media seriously challenged him. But at least here I focused on his legislative record, rather than his peculiar and sometimes reckless habits. Yet the Congressman will undoubtedly reveal his notoriously thin skin as a result of this column.

In the last congressional campaign, Mr. Frank found himself in the unusual position of being put on the defensive, and even uttered a falsehood that the 9/11 hijackers were here illegally. Yet of the 19 hijackers, all but three were here legally, and he knew it.

Because it was Barney Frank, after all, who made it possible for the 9/11 terrorists to legally enter—and remain in—the United States…which likely explains why he was recently dropped from the Congressional Committee on Homeland Security.
Letter: 'Give Rep. Frank a fair hearing'

Wednesday, April 27, 2005

Congressman Barney Frank has called Newton Tab columnist Tom Mountain a liar in his column "Mountain Lies" [April 20].

As his former political opponent, I have debated terrorism with the congressmen. Mountain writes in "Barney Frank's Role in 9/11" [April 13]: "Between 1981 and 2001, Barney Frank sponsored no less than 13 amendments to the Immigration and Nationality Act, which had the effect of opening the nation's floodgates to a well-disciplined, well-organized network of terrorist sleeper cells."

As Congress seeks to establish appropriate restrictions on illegal immigration this year, Frank's spurious record will come under further scrutiny.

Frank himself addressed the issue in "Barney Frank's Views on the Terrorism Bill": "The bill would have allowed the exclusion of visa applicants who had 'endorsed or espoused terrorist activity'…but the mere 'espousal or endorsement' of terrorist activity casts far too wide a net of exclusion."

Gerald Posner, in his New York Times bestseller "Why America Slept" wrote: "Congressman Barney Frank…led a successful effort to amend the Immigration and Nationality Act so that membership in a terrorist group was no longer sufficient to deny a visa.

"Under Frank's amendment, which seems unthinkable post 9/11, a visa could only be denied if the government could prove that the applicant had committed an act of terrorism."

Former Clinton CIA director James Woolsey wrote in the Wall Street Journal: "Congress had made it illegal to deny visas to members of terrorist groups."

The practical result was that members of Hamas, Hizbollah, and the Sept. 11 hijackers, no longer excluded because of their political views, arrived in droves in the 1990's, according to terrorism expert Steven Emerson.

Others have noted that Frank blundered by sponsoring this legislation. Are they all lying?

Why not set the record straight? I am requesting a formal Congressional inquiry into the matter. I'm certain that Congressman Frank's colleagues in Congress will provide him with a full and fair hearing.

My request for an investigation, sent to the Honorable F. James Sensenbrenner, chairman of the Judiciary Committee, is posted on my Web site www.chuck-morse.com .

Chuck Morse

Letter: Frank's 'angry, un-American agenda'

Wednesday, April 27, 2005

Dear Barney Frank,

This is America. In America we value freedom of speech but not character assassination. I am disgusted by your repulsive language. Facts are facts: You no longer serve on the Homeland Security Committee because of a technicality and I feel safer because of it. I hope and pray you never serve on it again. The McCarthy Era is history however political ideologues never fade away. Why do you work so hard to make it easier for foreigners who want to terrorize us to enter our country and live amongst us? How many foreign nationals live in your district? You just don't like that Tom Mountain caught you trying to unravel what our country stands for. You owe Mr. Mountain an apology for calling him a liar and other names. Who do you think you are? John Kerry? Teresa? Just because you personally have never abided by the laws of our land doesn't mean you can twist other laws to suit your angry, un-American agenda. I don't know about New Bedford or Fall River but have you forgotten that terrorists lived right here in Newton on the eve of 9-11? Your unnatural interest in loosening the restrictions on immigration is mysterious and frightening. Maybe you think we got what we deserved on 9-11? Tom Mountain did his research and reported his conclusions about you. I've never known him to be of anything but the highest integrity. I thank God for our immigration laws, for every Tom Mountain, the Minutemen, our military, the USA Patriot Act and our Constitution. America-haters must be prohibited from entering our country and immediately deported upon discovery. What kind of political ideologue are you? One who aids and abets the enemy? I will never vote for you again.

Mary Clossey

Letter: Morse, Posner are still wrong

Wednesday, May 4, 2005

Charles Morse has apparently decided to speak directly rather than as Tom Mountain's ventriloquist.

He repeats Gerald Posner's assertion that my amendment said "a visa could only be denied if the government could prove that the applicant had committed an act of terrorism."

But as Mr. Morse knows, Mr. Posner is wrong. Here is the language: "Any alien who (I) has engaged in a terrorist activity, or (II) a consular officer or the Attorney General knows, or has reasonable ground to believe, is likely to engage after entry in any terrorist activity (as defined in clause (iii)), is excludable."

Posner/Morse Error #1: The government does not have to "prove" anything; it has to have a "reasonable ground to believe" that there would be a problem.

Posner/Morse Error #2: What the government has to have reason to believe is not that the applicant had committed an act of terrorism, but only that he or she was likely to commit such an act in the future.

Mr. Morse continues to ignore 9/11 Commission Chairman Tom Kean's specific denial that this language led to the admission of the 9/11 murderers.

Facts having failed him, Mr. Morse now asks the Judiciary Committee to investigate my work. The suggestion that the committee on which I served for 22 years will now learn something by investigating me makes sense only to someone as ideologically besotted as he is. (If I were to be investigated, my co-investigatees would be Senator Alan Simpson and the late Senator Daniel Patrick Moynihan, the active cosponsors of what I did in this particular area.)

Rep. Barney Frank

Newton

APPENDIX B

Data for this report compiled from various news sources and checked where possible against official sources including the Dec. 2002 Senate report "Joint inquiry into Intelligence Community Activities Before and After the Terrorist Attacks of September 11, 2001" (Released in July 2003) and the Feb. 2004 Staff Report of the National Commission on Terrorist Attacks. Updated 2/04.

According to authorities, all of the hijackers who committed the September 11, 2001 terrorist attacks were foreigners. All of them entered the country legally on a temporary visa, mostly tourist visas with entry permits for six months. Although four of them attended flight school in the United States, only one is known to have entered on an appropriate visa for such study, and one entered on an F-1 student visa. Besides the four pilots, all but one of the terrorists entered the United States only once and had been in the country for only three to five months before the attacks. The four pilots had been in the United States for extended periods, although none was a legal permanent resident. Some had received more than one temporary visa, most of which were currently valid on September 11, but at least three of them had fallen out of status and were, therefore, in the United States illegally. The terrorists had obtained U.S. identification that was used for boarding flights in the form of Florida, Virginia, California and New Jersey driver's licenses/ID cards. One of the terrorists, Mohamed Atta, was detained in Florida for driving without a license, but subsequently obtained one. Thirteen of the terrorists had Florida driver's licenses or ID cards, seven had Virginia driver's licenses, at least two had California licenses and two had New Jersey driver's licenses. According to the March 28, 2002 Pittsburgh Post-Gazette, Robert Thibadeau, director of Carnegie Mellon's Internet Security laboratory, says that "the 19 terrorists on Sept. 11 were holding 63 state driver's licenses for identification." In the probe of the attack, numerous other people with potential connections to the hijackings have been detained for immigration violations.[Note: In the conversion of names from the Arabic alphabet into ours, there is no single correct spelling. This is why the names of the terrorists vary in their spelling in different news accounts, and why computerized databases will not recognize the name when it is spelled differently from how it was entered into the database. For example, Mohamed could be spelled Muhamed or Mohammed, and al-Suami could be spelled Alsuami or al Swami, etc.]

The Pentagon Plane (AA Flight 77, Dulles to Los Angeles)

    1. Hani Hasan Hanjour (26)—Saudi Arabian—pilot

- First came to U.S. in Oct. 1991 to study English in Tucson, Arizona.

- Had been in U.S. in April 1996, when he lived in Oakland, Cal. where he studied English, and later received flight training in Scottsdale, Arizona. He left in Nov. 1996 and returned again in Nov. 1997 while he obtained a FAA commercial pilot certificate. He left again in April 1999.

- Obtained student visa (F-1) in Jeddah, Saudi Arabia in Sept. 2000 after an initial refusal. According to the 2/04 Staff Report of the National Commission on Terrorist Attacks, Hanjour failed to reveal in his visa application that he had previously traveled to the United States.

- Returned Dec. 2000 to study English at Holy Names College (Oakland CA) but never showed up at the school. In illegal status because he did not enroll, and his entry permit had expired at the time of the attack.

- Lived in San Diego, Phoenix and Mesa, Ariz. (with Nawaf al-Hamzi), and later in Northern Virginia.

- Had a Virginia driver's license.

    2. Khalid al-Mihdhar (or Almidhar)—Saudi Arabian

- Obtained U.S. tourist visa in Jeddah, Saudi Arabia in April 1999.

- In Malaysia in Jan. 2000. Followed by Malaysian agents tipped off by CIA (see Wash. Post 2/3/02).

- Arrived at Los Angeles Jan. 15, 2000 with Nawaf al-Hamzi on B-2 tourist visa from Malaysia.

- Lived in San Diego, where he took flight training in May 2000 with Nawaf al-Hamzi.

- Left U.S. in June 2000 and obtained new B-1 visa in Saudi Arabia. According to the 2/04 Staff Report of the National Commission on Terrorist Attacks, his application falsely indicated he had not previously traveled to the United States and contained "suspicious indicators." It also revealed that he had more than one passport.

- Returned July 4, 2001, lived in New York.
- Put on the <u>Watch List for terrorists in August 2001 after entering U.S. last time.</u>
- In legal nonimmigrant status at the time of the attack.
- Had a Virginia driver's license.

3. Nawaf al-Hamzi (or Alhamzi)—Saudi Arabian (brother of Salem)

- Obtained U.S. tourist visa in Jeddah, Saudi Arabia in April 1999. According to the 2/04 Staff Report of the National Commission on Terrorist Attacks, his application contained "suspicious indicators."
- In Malaysia in Jan. 2000. <u>Followed by Malaysian agents tipped off by CIA</u> (see Wash. Post 2/3/02).
- Arrived at Los Angeles Jan. 15, 2000 with al-Midhar from Malaysia.
- Lived in San Diego, where he took flight training in May 2000 with al-Midhar, in Dec. 2000 moved to Mesa Arizona (with Hani Hanjour), and later to Fort Lee, N.J., Wayne, N.J. and Northern Virginia.
- Applied to INS July 12, 2000 for extension of permitted stay in U.S. (apparently granted for additional six months).
- Put on the <u>Watch List for terrorists in August 2001.</u> (with al-Mihdhar)
- Had been in <u>illegal visa overstay status for nine months at the time of the attack.</u>
- Had California, Florida and Virginia driver's licenses.

4. Salem al-Hamzi (or Alhamzi)—Saudi Arabian (brother of Nawaf)

- Obtained U.S. tourist visa in Jeddah, Saudi Arabia in April 1999.
- Arrived U.S. June 2001.
- Lived in Fort Lee, N.J., Wayne, N.J.

- In legal nonimmigrant status at the time of the attack.
- Had a Virginia driver's license.

5. Majed Moqed—Saudi Arabian

- Identity in doubt.
- Entered on tourist visa obtained in Saudi Arabia after May 2001.
- In legal nonimmigrant status at the time of the attack.
- Had a Virginia driver's license.

The WTC North Tower Plane (AA Flight 11, Boston to Los Angeles)

1. Mohamed Atta—Egyptian (43)—pilot

- Born in Egypt in 1968.
- Graduated from Cairo Univ. with degree in Architectural Engineering in 1990.
- Obtained visitor visa in Berlin Germany, May 2000.
- Entered U.S. at Newark on June 3, 2000 on tourist visa and given entry permit until December 2, 2000.
- Applied in Sept. 2000 to INS for change in status to trainee.
- Attended Huffman Aviation School in Venice Florida with al-Shehhi.
- Arrested in Florida for driving without license, and failed to show up for court date—bench warrant issued.
- Subsequently obtained Florida driver's license.
- Obtained FAA pilot's certificate.
- According to the 2/04 Staff Report of the National Commission on Terrorist Attacks, had overstayed his entry permit as of Dec. 4, 2000.
- Flew to Madrid Jan. 2001.
- United Arab Emirate (UAE) authorities state Atta detained in January 2001 on basis of his name appearing on terrorist alert list, but was not held in absence of U.S. charges. UAE states that U.S. authorities were warned Atta intended to return to U.S.

- Returned to U.S. on January 10, 2001 at Miami and was sent to secondary inspection because he acknowledged being in flight training but did not have required trainee visa. Interagency Border Information System (IBIS) database checked. Admitted by INS based on pending application for change to trainee status.

- Moved to Georgia in Jan. 2001 for additional flight training with al-Shehhi.

- Left U.S. and returned from Madrid on July 19, 2001 and <u>given permission to stay until November 2, 2001</u>.

- Also lived in Hollywood and Coral Springs, Fla.

- Received change of status approval by INS in September a year after the attacks.

2. Satam al-Suqami (25)—Saudi Arabian

- Obtained business visa in Saudi Arabia (but was residing in United Arab Emirates).

- Entered U.S. in May 2001. According to the 2/04 Staff Report of the National Commission on Terrorist Attacks, asked for and was admitted for 20 days and was in overstay status at the time of the attacks. The Commission staff also said his passport was doctored (presumably with pages removed to hide his travel to countries where he obtained terrorist training).

- <u>Was in overstay status at the time of the attack.</u>

3. Waleed al-Shehri (or Alshehri) (21)—Saudi Arabian (brother of Wail)

- Obtained tourist visa in Saudi Arabia.

- Entered U.S. in May 2000.

- Licensed pilot.

- Lived in Hollywood, Orlando and Daytona Beach (all in Florida).

- In <u>illegal nonimmigrant status (visa overstay)</u> at time of the attack.

- Had a Florida driver's license.

4. Wail (or Wael) al-Shehri (or Alshehri) (25)—Saudi Arabian (brother of Waleed)

- Obtained tourist visa in Saudi Arabia.

- Lived in Hollywood, Fla. and Newton, Mass.

- Had a Florida ID card.

5. Abdulaziz al-Omari (or Alomari)—Saudi Arabian

- Obtained tourist visa in Saudi Arabia in June 2001.

- According to the 2/04 Staff Report of the National Commission on Terrorist Attacks, his passport was doctored (presumably with pages removed to hide his travel to countries where he obtained terrorist training).

- In legal nonimmigrant status at the time of the attack.

- Lived in Hollywood, Fla.

- Had a Florida and Virginia driver's licenses.

The WTC South Tower Plane (UA Flight 175, Boston to Los Angeles)

1. Marwan al-Shehhi (or Alshehhi)—United Arab Emirates—pilot

- Studied electrical engineering at Tech. Univ. in Hamburg.

- In January 2000, obtained 10-year, multiple entry tourist visa in Dubai, United Arab Emirates.

- Entered the U.S. in May 2000, applied September for change of status to student.

- Attended flight school in Florida, obtained FAA pilot's certificate.

- Took at least 3 trips out of U.S. and back. (Overstayed entry permit as of Nov. 2000, left U.S. in Dec. 2000, returned Jan. 2001.)

- Attended flight school in Georgia with Atta in Jan. 2001. According to the 2/04 Staff Report of the National Commission on Terrorist Attacks, was sent to secondary inspection, but was admitted.)

- Flew to Egypt April 8, 2001, returned from Morocco May 2, 2001.
- In legal nonimmigrant status at the time of the attack.
- Lived in New York City area, Georgia and moved to Hollywood, Fla. in July with Atta and trained at Huffman Aviation in Venice.
- Had a Florida driver's license.

2. Fayez Ahmed Rashid Ahmed al-Qadi Banihammad (aka Fayez Ahmed)—United Arab Emirates

- Obtained tourist visa in United Arab Emirates.
- Entered U.S. in June.
- Lived in Delray Beach, Fla.

3. Ahmed al-Ghamdi (or Alghamdi)—Saudi Arabian

- Obtained tourist visa in Saudi Arabia.
- Entered U.S. in May.
- In <u>illegal visa overstay status at the time of the attack.</u>
- Lived in Delray Beach, Fla.
- Had a Florida ID card.
- Had a Virginia driver's license

4. Hamza Saleh al-Ghamdi (or Alghamdi) (20)—Saudi Arabian

- Obtained visa in Saudi Arabia.
- Lived in Delray Beach, Fla.
- Had a Florida driver's license.

5. Mohand al-Shehri (or Alshehri)—Saudi Arabian

- Identity in doubt.
- Obtained tourist visa in Saudi Arabia.
- Admitted to U.S. in May.
- Lived in Delray Beach, Fla.

<u>The Pennsylvania Plane (UA Flight 93, Newark to San Francisco)</u>

    1. Ziad Samir Jarrah—Lebanese—pilot

- Born in Lebanon in 1975.

- Studied aircraft construction and maintenance at Hamburg tech. univ. 1996-00.

- Obtained five-year, multiple-entry tourist visa in Germany.

- Entered U.S. in June 27, 2000 at Atlanta.

- Trained as a pilot in Venice, Florida and Virginia Gardens, Florida but never obtained student trainee visa. Received FAA pilot's certificate.

- Took at least 5 trips out of U.S. and back (flew to Germany July 25 and returned August 5, 2001).

- Lived in Delray Beach, Fla.

- In legal nonimmigrant status at the time of the attack.

- Had a Florida driver's license.

    2. Saeed al-Ghamdi (or Alghamdi)—Saudi Arabian

- Identity in doubt.

- Obtained tourist visa in Saudi Arabia. According to the 2/04 Staff Report of the National Commission on Terrorist Attacks, application falsely stated he had not previously applied for a U.S. visa.

- Entered U.S. in June 2001. According to the 2/04 Staff Report of the National Commission on Terrorist Attacks, he was sent to secondary inspection, because he had a one-way ticket and $500, but was admitted.

- Lived in Delray Beach, Fla.

- Had a Florida ID card.

    3. Ahmed Ibrahim A. al-Haznawi (or Alhaznawi) (21)—Saudi Arabian

- Obtained tourist visa in Saudi Arabia.

- Entered the U.S. in June 2001. According to the 2/04 Staff Report of the National Commission on Terrorist Attacks, his passport may have had "suspicious indicators."
- In legal nonimmigrant status at the time of the attack.
- Lived in Delray Beach, Fla.
- Had a Florida driver's license.

4. Ahmed Abdullah al-Nami (or Alnami) (23)—Saudi Arabian

- Obtained tourist visa in Saudi Arabia.
- Entered the U.S. in May 2001. According to the 2/04 Staff Report of the National Commission on Terrorist Attacks, his passport may have had "suspicious indicators."
- In legal nonimmigrant status at the time of the attack.
- Lived in Delray Beach, Fla.
- Had a Florida ID card.

Other Conspirators:

- Khalid Sheikh Mohamed (Coordinator)—Indicted in 1996 in N.Y. for his role in an earlier terrorist plot. Had a Saudi Arabian passport (although not a Saudi national)—obtained a U.S. visa in July 2001.
- Ramzi Bin-al-shibh—Yemeni (potential pilot)—denied visa four times.
- Zakariya Essabar—Moroccan—potential pilot/hijacker—denied visa.
- Saeed "Jihad" al Gamdi—Potential hijacker—denied visa.
- Ali Abdul Aziz Ali—Pakistani—finacial facilitator—denied visa.
- Mohamed al Kahtani—potential hijacker—denied visa.

Notes

Aiding and Abetting

   1. H.R. 4427 Introduced 4/20/1988

Title: A bill to amend the Immigration and Nationality Act with respect to the grounds for exclusion and deportation of aliens'….Repeals the ideological grounds for exclusion.

   H.R.1119 Introduced 2/18/1987
Title: A bill to amend the Immigration and Nationality Act with respect to the grounds for exclusion and deportation of aliens.

H.R.1280 Introduced 3/7/1989
Title: To amend the Immigration and Nationality Act with respect to grounds for exclusion and deportation of aliens. Repeals the ideological grounds for exclusion.

2. Mark Riebling, Wedge: From Pearl Harbor to 9/11—The Secret War between the FBI and the CIA, 1994 pp. 434-437:

FBI and CIA had been trying to coordinate in denying visas to some of these would-be terrorists since September 1986, when the agencies joined an Alien Border Control Committee (ABCC)…But after the Agency tips led the Bureau to arrest eight suspected Palestinian terrorists in Los Angeles in early 1987, civil-liberty activists pressured the ABCC to drop a plan to systematize use of CIA intelligence in processing visa requests. Congressman Barney Frank then led a successful movement to amend the Immigration and Nationality Act, so that membership in terrorist groups would no longer be sufficient grounds for the denial of visas…The United States therefore had no obvious grounds for refusing visas to radicals such as…Sheikh Omar Abdel Rahman, leader of the Islamic Jidhad.

3. H.R.3305 Introduced 10/19/1993
Title: To amend the Immigration and Nationality Act to establish a Board of Visa Appeals within the Department of State to review decisions of consular officers concerning visa applications, revocations and cancellations.

Murthy.com—the law office of Sheela Murthy, Immigration Law

Consular Review Bill Introduced Again
Posted Apr 20, 1999
A Bill to establish a Board of Visa Appeals to review decisions of Consular Officers on visa matters, has again been introduced in the House of Representatives. Congressman Frank of Massachusetts has proposed this Bill, a favorite of immigration attorneys, including at the Law Office of Sheela Murthy, repeatedly over the years. Every time, of course, the Bill meets strong opposition from the Department of State.
Authors comment: The judgment of the embassy official or indirect evidence of a connection to terrorism would not be enough to deny a visa under this law. Terrorist hijacker Mohammad Atta was granted a visitor's visa at the American Embassy in Berlin on June 3, 1999.

H.R.2975 Introduced 2/27/1996
Title: To amend the Immigration and Nationality Act to establish a Board of Visa Appeals within the Department of State to review decisions of consular officers concerning visa applications, revocations and cancellations.

H.R.4539 Introduced 9/10/1998
Title: To amend the Immigration and Nationality Act to establish a Board of Visa Appeals within the Department of State to review decisions of consular officers concerning visa applications, revocations and cancellations.

H.R. 1156 Introduced 3/17/1999
Title: To amend the Immigration and Nationality Act to establish a Board of Visa Appeals within the Department of State to review decisions of consular officers concerning visa applications, revocations, and cancellations.

H.R.1345 Introduced 4/3/2001

Title: To amend the Immigration and Nationality Act to establish a Board of Visa Appeals within the Department of State to review decisions of consular officers concerning visa applications, revocations, and cancellations.

4. H.R. 4509 Introduced 11/18/1983
Title: A bill to amend the Immigration and Nationality Act with respect to the grounds for exclusion and deportation of aliens.

This bill codifies into law several categories for exclusion that already existed in the law before the bill was crafted. The bill makes the following changes to the already existing law regarding which applicants for visas would be excludable:

4. any alien convicted of two or more offenses for which the aggregate sentences actually imposed were five years or more.

This would lower the bar with regard to visas for convicted criminals. This means that if the applicant had spent less than 5 years in prison, or was convicted of only one crime, than a visa could not be denied.

7. any alien deemed by the Attorney General as a probable security risk for certain specified reasons.

This would raise the bar in terms of what constituted a security risk. The Attorney General would have less discretion under this law as evidence would now have to be presented that would have to involve specified reasons for denying a visa as opposed to judgment, suspicion or second hand information. Under this rule, it would be more difficult to prove that the applicant was a security risk.

8. any alien who is an active member of an organization engaged in violence or terrorist activities.

What about inactive membership? What about indirect support or expressed sympathies? During the cold war years, the communists used to get around this by simply having their operatives not join the party. Certainly al Quada is not an organization in the formal sense with membership.
Makes deportable by the Attorney General only those aliens within one of the following classes: (9) any alien who at any time is convicted on any of various specified loyalty laws (e.g. sabotage, treason and sedition, selective service, etc..)

(12) any alien engaging in activity, which endangers the public safety or national security;

None of the 9/11 hijackers, none of the Hamas members operating in this country in the 1990's, were actively involved in sabotage. Treasonous and seditious activities are extremely difficult to prove. The hijackers and the Hamas members operated entirely, in fact quite scrupulously, within the color of the law while they engaged in their activities. They didn't engage in activities that could easily be discerned as endangering public safety or national security. Hamas sent money overseas to fund those activities in other countries and the 9/11 hijackers planned and waited until 9/11 before violating "various specified loyalty laws."

3. H.R. 5227 Introduced 3/22/1984
Title: A bill to amend the Immigration and Nationality Act with respect to the grounds for exclusion and deportation of aliens.

This act is virtually identical to H.R. 4509, filed 4 months previous except for the following provision:

Repeals provisions dealing with bond and conditions for admission for permanent residence for retarded, tubercular, and mentally ill aliens.

4. H.R.2361 Introduced 5/6/1985
Title: A bill to amend the Immigration and Nationality Act with respect to the grounds for exclusion and deportation of aliens.

This act is virtually identical with the one filed in 1984 except for the following relevant changes:

6. any alien who has engaged in terrorist activity against the United States or against a citizen of the United States.

8. any alien deemed by the Attorney General as a probable security risk for certain specified reasons, including terrorist activity.

14. any alien who has engaged in terrorist activity against the United States or against a citizen of the United States

5. H.R. 5287 Introduced 12/16/1981

> Title: A bill to amend the Immigration and Nationality Act with respect to aliens who seek to enter the United States to do research at colleges and universities…. within the definition of "aliens who are members of the teaching profession or who have exceptional ability in the sciences or the arts."

Frank championed the cause of liberalizing the issuance of student visas as far back as 1981. Indeed this was one of his first legislative initiatives in Congress.

6. Malkin, Michelle Invasion—How America Still Welcomes Terrorists, Criminals, and Other Foreign Menaces to Our Shores. Washington D.C. Regnery Publishing, Inc. 2002

H.R.3928 Introduced 7/31/1996

Title: To amend the Immigration and Nationality Act with respect to waiver of exclusion for certain excludable aliens.

Authors comment: During the campaign, the congressman explained that he sponsored the "Family Reunification Act" to deal with the truly unjust situation of a resident alien who might have been convicted of a crime but who had paid his debt to society and yet was being deported many years, even decades later. Legislation could've been crafted to deal with those very specific situations. The sweeping Frank bill, also help dangerous foreign criminals appeal their deportations after the system had undergone the laborious and expensive process of deporting them.

Opening the Floodgates

1. Posner, Gerald Why America Slept—The failure to prevent 9/11. New York: Ballantine Books 2003

2. Mark Riebling, Wedge: From Pearl Harbor to 9/11—The Secret War between the FBI and the CIA, 1994

While the Bureau began investigating Rahman and his followers, Egyptian intelligence repeatedly warned CIA officers about a growing Islamic fundamentalist network in the United States…the Agency told them it could not monitor the men, since counter terrorism in the U.S. was the province of the FBI…The Bureau did recruit an agent in Rahman's entourage—former

Egyptian army officer Emad Salem—but his access was limited. Legally, there was little the FBI could do...The Egyptians countered by openly criticizing the U.S. system, which seemed to give suspected terrorists a free hand simply because they crossed from CIA into FBI jurisdiction—a policy which could only encourage such deadly immigration. In fact, two more Rahman followers, Mahmad Muhammad Ajaj and Ramzi Ahmed Yousef, had already come to the U.S. from Peshwar in September 1992...Following the World Trade Center bombing, for which both men were indicted, the Bureau realized that some important background information on Ajaj, Youssef, and other Rahman followers had been provided by Egypt well beforehand and was simply sitting in CIA databases.

It took the thousands of deaths on Sept 11, 2001 to get the U.S. government to free the FBI to visit Internet sites, libraries, churches and political organizations as part of an effort to give the beleaguered agency new tools to pre-empt terrorist strikes. Before this these actions including web surfing which any private citizen can do, had to be part of an ongoing criminal investigation. In other words a private citizen could investigate more easily on the web than the FBI. A lot of the investigating Steve Emerson did that led to his documentary "Jihad in America" was off limits to the FBI.

3. National Security Decision Directive #207—issues January 20, 1986

4. Ibid

5. Los Angeles Times—David G. Savage, The Great Alien Lockout

6. Posner

7. The Peoples Daily World—Who's blocking the free flow of ideas?—By Chuck Idelson

8. Steven Emerson—testimony before the Senate Judiciary Committee's Subcommittee on Terrorism, Technology, and Government Information—February 24, 1998

9. Ibid

10. Ibid

11. Ibid

12. Ibid.

13. Ibid

14. Protecting America-Law Enforcement views Radical Islam, Oliver Revell—Middle East Quarterly March 1995.

The Aftermath
1. The 9/11 Commission Report—Final Report of the National Commission on Terrorist Attacks Upon the United States.
Information in this chapter is largely extrapolated from the 9/11 Commission Report.

Conclusion

1. Mark Riebling, Wedge: Rahman entered the U.S. in May 1990…After New York police arrested one of Rahman's followers, El Sayyid Nosair, in connection with the killing of right-wing Israeli leader Rabbi Meir Kahane in November 1990, the FBI was intrigued to learn that Nosair's legal bills were paid and his family supported by Rahman.

2. The 9/11 Commission Report—Final Report of the National Commission on Terrorist Attacks Upon the United States

3. Reibling: By 1999, meanwhile, the annual spy budget, adjusted for inflation, was less than three-fourths of what it had been in 1989. Scarce Pentagon and CIA resources were diverted into questionable new areas such as "environmental intelligence," to counter, "green menaces" like elephant poaching.

If you would like to interview Chuck Morse, please contact him at:

Morse for Congress Committee
258 Harvard Street Suite 240
Brookline, MA 02446
1-800-272-7324
www.morseforcongress.com

Index

978-0-595-35948-6
0-595-35948-5

www.ingramcontent.com/pod-product-compliance
Lightning Source LLC
Chambersburg PA
CBHW020350290526
45785CB00005B/2220